DEDICATION

To all those women who love to create beautiful things and share them with the people they care about.

Sharing Scones and More

35 delightful recipes to share with the ones you love

with stories, inspirational thoughts, and tips

Beverly Pogue and Rosalie Clarke

CFI
Springville, UT

ISBN: 1-55517-845-5
e.1

Published by Cedar Fort, Inc.
www.cedarfort.com

Distributed by:

Cover and interior designed by Nicole Williams
Cover design © 2005 by Lyle Mortimer

Printed in the United States of America
10 9 8 7 6 5 4 3 2 1

Printed on acid-free paper

CONTENTS

THANKS AND . . .

To my husband, Mitchell, and our children—Lee, Brandon, Jordan, and Rachael—for taste-testing scone after scone after scone and for being my best fans.

To Mom, for "caving in" and sharing the stories.

To Chelli, for the balloons.

To Dad, for looking sideways.

And to my brothers, for giving me the reason to learn how to bake in the first place.

My gratitude for all of it.

Beverly Pogue

. . . ACKNOWLEDGMENTS

My daughter, Beverly, is a very persuasive lady. Her enthusiasm oozed out like melting honey butter on a hot scone straight from the oven, and before I knew it I was trapped in the project just as her Dad had trapped her into working The Puyallup. Conjuring old memories is an enjoyable and rewarding experience.

I have appreciated the encouragement given by my friends Joann Scott and Garry Morris, and I thank them for their gentle critiquing.

Thankfully, my husband, Al, has been patient throughout.

Despite my whining, I enjoyed the work and look forward to the next project.

Rosalie Clarke

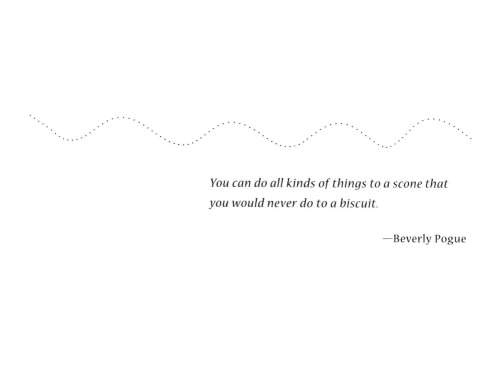

You can do all kinds of things to a scone that you would never do to a biscuit.

—Beverly Pogue

INTRODUCTION

One of the greatest strengths of women is our desire and willingness to share with one another—a pot of soup when someone is ill, a note of encouragement at just the right time, a vase of flowers, or a favorite recipe. Such acts are physical manifestations of our desire to help. With these seemingly small things, we express sympathy, gratitude, empathy, and love. We are saying, "I know how you feel. I was in that situation once myself. I want you to be successful. I want you to be happy."

In the spirit of sharing, we offer here a collection of stories, recipes, tips, and sayings we hope will be both enjoyable and beneficial. Either learned ourselves or passed on to us by others, they have become who we are, enriching our daily lives and enhancing our strengths as women.

Best regards,

Beverly Pogue & Rosalie Clarke

Scone *[Scot. skon]—n. a small, rich, biscuit-like quick bread, Scottish in origin, usually triangular in shape, and traditionally served split and buttered for tea.*

WHAT'S A SCONE?

"Excuse me," said a well-dressed woman just outside the window to our booth. "But what's a scone?"

I had to laugh at the confused look on her face. We were just outside the Red Gate at the fairgrounds in Puyallup, Washington, where the fall fair was in full swing. More than a million people come to "Do The Puyallup" each year, and for seventeen days every September this city becomes a very busy place. The downtown is packed, the traffic is outrageous, the motels and restaurants are full, and we love it.

The school children love it because each student gets a free ticket to the fair and half a day off to go. The rest of us love it because the fair is a chance to not only have a great time but also to earn some extra dollars. We get jobs inside the fairgrounds, or we set up vending booths and sell things outside the fairgrounds. People, schools, and nearby churches sell parking spaces all over their lawns or grounds. If there is a place a car can fit, there will be someone waving you into it. If there is something you might buy, there is someone ready to offer you the opportunity.

And my father is one of them.

Dad owns one of the corner lots outside the fairgrounds, and during the fair he rents part of the ground to other individuals to put their booths where they sell food or other items. He uses the rest of the space for his own booths, gradually expanding from selling hot dogs and hamburgers to curly fries and cotton candy. Each year he takes note of what works and what doesn't and adjusts accordingly. This year the new thing was selling scones. And he wanted *me* to be his baker.

That's when *I* was the one who asked, "What's a scone?"

TRAPPED

If I had grown up with Dad or had lived in the Puget Sound area long enough, I would have known what a scone was. But I hadn't, and so I didn't. I had been raised by my mother and grew up in the cherry orchards of The Dalles, Oregon. There my baking specialties became homemade breads and cookies. I had graduated from high school, lived with Dad and his family for a short time, and eventually wound up in Utah, where I married my husband and began a family. Four children, many moves, and many years later found us back in the Puget Sound area, living in the city of Puyallup.

"We're making scones this year for the fair," Dad said one day, looking sideways at me. "Know where we can find a baker?"

While I didn't know about scones, I *did* know about selling things at the fair. I hadn't worked in any of Dad's booths, but I had *seen* others working, and they worked hard and fast. They dealt with a lot of people, stood on their feet almost all day, and ran nonstop for the duration of The Puyallup, often not being able to leave until one in the morning. I had heard stories from Dad over the years and had seen his booths in action a few times, and I wanted no part of it. Sauntering was more my style. These people *sprinted*! It was intimidating.

I laughed as if he were joking and asked him some polite questions about his latest idea, while the realization grew in me that I was trapped. Dad was going to finagle me into being his baker and there wasn't anything I could do about it. And he didn't even care that I'd never made a scone.

A SCONE IS. . .

A scone (as I was eventually able to explain to our confused fairgoer) is like a biscuit, only sweeter. A fair scone is made from a mix with water added to it. We dump a few pounds of the mix into the mixer, add the proper amount of water, and blend for a few seconds. The resulting dough is then scooped out of the mixing bowl, kneaded briefly on a floured counter, divided into eight-ounce balls, and lightly kneaded again until smooth.

(Everything having to do with scones is all about "briefly" or "lightly"—especially if you're working the fair—or "quickly.")

It's easier to do the next part if the balls of dough have a chance to rest for a bit, but most of the time there *is* no time.

With our hand in a slightly cupped shape, we pat or press or (lightly) pound the dough out into a 6½- to 7-inch circle. The idea is to have a circle of dough with a slight mound in the middle. Each circle is cut to make four triangular or wedge-shaped pieces, which are placed at least an inch apart on an ungreased baking sheet. We bake the scones in a commercial convection oven at 375 degrees Fahrenheit for 10–12 minutes or until lightly browned.

(The next part is a bit tricky, and I never did get the hang of it. Unfortunately, I *did* get the hang of mixing, shaping, and timing the baking well enough that no one was willing to fire me.)

The scones are allowed to cool just enough to where we can handle them without being burned. (Latex gloves and heat don't go well together.) Each scone is sliced in half horizontally with a knife, from the narrow tip of the scone to within half an inch of the wide back. The scone is carefully opened just enough to be able to slather honey butter and raspberry jam in the middle. It is then bagged and ready for the fairgoer to buy.

And buy them they did. In the rain (which falls a lot in the Pacific Northwest), in the sun, as soon as we opened, and after we wanted to close, people bought scones. At one point, while we were making scones as fast as possible, Dad put his hands on my shoulders and said, "Look behind you." I turned to see a line of customers stretching out away from our booth and into the street. What was worse (or better, depending on the perspective) they weren't buying one or two scones, they were buying dozens!

The locals discovered our convenient location (on a busy road on their way to work) and wanted us to have scones ready before 6 A.M. *Real* fair scones are only available in our area during fair time, and people seemed to want to get their fill of scones while they had the chance. And taking a sack-full to the office to go with the morning coffee would be a great way to make points with co-workers.

While we would have liked to oblige them, this was a case of the "spirit being willing but the flesh being weak." A person has to get some sleep *sometime*.

After seventeen days the fair was finally over. The parking lots emptied, the traffic went back to normal, the booths came down, and the vending trailers were towed away. Dad paid everyone, we said our good-byes, and we were done.

But I wasn't. Dad had started something that wasn't stopping. I had become fascinated with the art of making scones, and I was determined to learn more.

—Beverly Pogue

Trying to do a task that you're afraid of can be good for you. You end up with something— skills, experience, and knowledge—you can share that you didn't have before.

OLD RECIPE BOX

This brings my Mother closer to me now
Than pen or portrait—just this faded book.
Only ingredients are listed here: not how
To mix them. I can see her reproachful look:
'Why, you remember that, my child, for certain!'
I can hear her saying: 'That one is from Mabel!'
I recall sun sifting through a gingham curtain
Making a stained-glass cover for the table.
I use these recipes now over and over:
Fat biscuit, short-cake, and top-heavy loaves
Of golden-crusted bread as sweet as clover,
And when the scent of cinnamon and cloves
Spice the warm air, those days return once more,
And memory consecrates each homely chore.

— Eleanor Alletta Chaffee
Found in Grandma's wooden recipe box

MAKING SCONES

Making scones at home from scratch is a bit different from making them at the fair from a mix. Here are a few tips that will help ensure your success.

INGREDIENTS

Because a scone *is* such a simple thing, it is important to use good ingredients. For this reason, unsalted butter is almost always preferred. You will also want to make sure that any extracts, nuts, or dried fruits are of high quality.

CUTTING IN THE BUTTER

Once you have the dry ingredients stirred together in a bowl, it is time to cut in the butter. The butter needs to be chilled and cut into pieces before adding to the flour mixture.

To cut the butter in with two knives, hold a knife in each hand. Make an X with the knives, put them tip down in the bowl, and draw the knives passed each other across the bowl to the opposite sides. Do this, turning the bowl, until the mixture looks like a coarse meal.

To cut the butter in with a pastry blender, hold the bowl firmly on the table with one hand and, with the other hand, push the pastry blender down through the flour mixture and slice it toward you with a rocking motion. Continue doing this, turning the bowl, until the mixture looks like a coarse meal.

To cut the butter in with a food processor, put the flour mixture in the food processor, add the butter, and do five to seven short pulses until the mixture looks like a coarse meal. Do not overmix. Then pour the flour mixture back in a bowl and continue with the recipe as directed.

MIXING, KNEADING, AND ROLLING THE DOUGH

Be gentle and keep a light touch. Too much mixing or kneading will produce a tough scone. Use a flat wooden spoon or rubber spatula to mix with folding or slicing motions. Knead without pushing hard. You only want to knead enough to form the dough into a ball that can be patted or rolled out and cut into the desired scone shapes.

If rolling the dough, do not push down hard. Roll to ¾-inch thick, cut out the scones with a floured cutter. Be sure to reknead, form, and roll the scraps with the same light touch.

SHAPING AND CUTTING THE DOUGH

Divide the dough into whatever amount of portions the recipe calls for. With your hand in a slightly cupped shape, lightly pat or press the dough out into a 6- to 6½ -inch circle. The idea is to have a circle of dough with a slight mound in the middle.

With a floured knife, cut the mounds into four, six, or eight equal wedges, depending on the size scone you want. Be aware that sometimes people will actually eat more if the scones are cut into smaller shapes. Many of the scone recipes are too rich to serve as large wedges.

BAKING THE SCONES

Preheat the oven 10–15 minutes before baking, and bake the scones on the center rack. I use an insulated cookie sheet to ensure the bottoms do not brown more quickly than the tops. Remember it is not necessary to grease the cookie sheet.

EATING A SCONE

Most of us do not do tea English style, so we don't know the "proper" way to eat a scone. I must admit that I am inclined to eat them as I would a biscuit. Often I will not even put anything on them but rather will eat them plain.

If you would like to eat a scone in a more genteel fashion, then cut the scone horizontally in half with a tea knife. Put a spoonful of jam, Mock Devonshire cream, or lemon curd on your tea plate. (Do not take the spreads directly from their containers and directly to your scone.) Spread a bit of jam or lemon curd on a small portion only of your scone and top with the Mock Devonshire cream. Take a bite and then repeat.

FREEZING SCONES

There is no doubt that scones taste best warm from the oven. To make life a little easier in the mornings or to be prepared for company at any time, make the scones but do not bake. Instead put them on a cookie sheet and flash-freeze them. Once the scones are frozen, you can transfer them to a plastic bag or an airtight container and store up to four weeks in the freezer.

When you are ready to bake the scones, remove the desired amount from the freezer and put them on an ungreased cookie sheet. Turn on the oven to preheat for fifteen minutes. By then the scones will be thawed enough to bake according to directions (usually at about 375 degrees Fahrenheit for 12–15 minutes).

IDEAS FOR SHARING

Unique and beautiful, scones are good candidates for gift-giving. Arrange them on breakfast trays, vintage plates, or in cloth-lined bowls or baskets. Add your favorite jams or jellies, specialty cheeses, or fruits. Some packets of teas, cider, or hot chocolate make a nice addition, along with the scone recipe on a card.

My sister-in-law, Chelli, a talented gift giver, recommends two things: 1) Wrap your gift baskets in cellophane (because "every gift basket looks better in cellophane"), and 2) Don't be shy about being thoughtful. "When a friend is sad and gets a gift," she says, "she'll know she is not alone. It's a good way to help."

CLOTHESPINS

One of the nicest odors available to the homemaker is the smell of sheets and pillowcases dried outside. The smell lingers long after they are placed in the cupboard and, for those of us who are older, it conjures many memories. Mine is of sitting at the oilcloth-covered table eating Campbell's tomato soup and toasted cheese sandwiches while my mother washed clothes in the kitchen in the older wringer washing machine. My dad had made benches of just the right height to hold the washtubs with the rinse water, and after going back and forth through the wringer and rinse water and wringer again, the wash (still heavy with water because there was no spin cycle) was taken in an oilcloth-lined basket out to the clotheslines behind the garage and hung in the sunshine.

Anyone who hangs out wash knows that there are two kinds of clothespins. One is the pinch kind with the spring in the middle. They all eventually come apart, and the pieces fly everywhere.

The clothespins of my youth (still available in nostalgia shops) were the push type. Hanging wash on the line can be an aesthetic few minutes. No one with an ounce of artistic sensibility would ever hang wash the way it is done in the western movies. My goodness, we are hanging the wash to dry, not just putting it on the line in a glob!

Shake out towels with a snap, and pin them neatly to the line all in a row. Hang shirts upside down with a clothespin at each side seam and one in the middle to hold the two front halves together. You will find fewer wrinkles to press out when they dry. And if you are fortunate enough to have the old push pins, notice the music they make as they are pushed over the wet fabric. Every time I hear that sound, I can see the oilcloth-covered table, taste the tomato soup and cheese sandwiches, hear the motor of the old washing machine, and feel the sun on my face as I help my mother hang the heavy wash on the line.

Rosalie Clarke

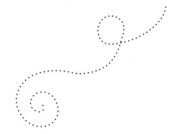

SIMPLE SCONES

Do what you can. And as you do what you can, what you can't do will get smaller.

SCOTTISH SCONES

A plain scone, using the most basic ingredients.

2½ cups all-purpose flour

1 tbsp. baking powder

¼ tsp. salt

4 tbsp. unsalted butter or
    margarine, chilled and cut
    into pieces

1 cup milk

Preheat oven to 450 degrees Fahrenheit.

Combine dry ingredients in a medium-sized bowl. Add butter and cut into the flour mixture with a pastry blender or two knives to make a coarse meal. Add the milk and stir just until it forms a dough ball. Knead lightly and briefly on a floured surface. Divide the dough into four equal portions. Shape each portion into a ball and let rest 2–3 minutes.

Pat each ball into a 4½-round, slightly mounded, and cut into 4 wedges. Put on an ungreased baking sheet.

Bake 8–10 minutes or until golden brown. Cool on a wire cooling rack for 5 minutes. Serve warm with butter and jam. Makes 16 cute, fat scones.

IRISH SODA SCONES

This scone is like a biscuit but without the baking powder aftertaste. And because it is not sweet, it makes a good background for butter and the jam of your choice.

1½ cups all-purpose flour

½ tsp. baking soda

½ tsp. cream of tartar

¼ tsp. salt

4 tbsp. margarine, chilled and

  cut into pieces

½ cup buttermilk

1 tbsp. water

Preheat oven to 375 degrees Fahrenheit.

Combine dry ingredients in a medium-sized bowl. Add margarine and cut into the flour mixture with a pastry blender or two knives to make a coarse meal. In a separate bowl combine the buttermilk and water. Add to the dry ingredients and mix just until blended.

Turn the dough onto a floured surface and knead lightly. Roll out to ½-inch thick and cut into rounds with a 2-inch floured biscuit cutter.

Place on an ungreased baking sheet, allowing an inch or more between each scone.

Bake 10 minutes or until golden. Serve warm with butter and jam. Makes approximately 10 scones.

I~HAVE~NO~BUTTERMILK SCONES

This scone works well as a wedge and is pretty as a round. Definitely use the glaze for a shiny top.

2 cups all-purpose flour

1/3 cup granulated sugar

2 tsp. baking powder

1/8 tsp. salt

1/3 cup unsalted butter, chilled
   and cut into pieces

1 large egg

1 tsp. vanilla extract

1/2 cup milk

Glaze:

1 egg white, slightly beaten

Preheat oven to 375 degrees Fahrenheit.

Combine dry ingredients in a medium-sized bowl. Add butter and cut into the flour mixture with a pastry blender or two knives to make a coarse meal. In a separate bowl combine the large egg, vanilla extract, and milk. Add to the dry ingredients and mix quickly, just until blended. Turn the dough onto a floured board or cloth and knead lightly a few times. To make wedges, divide the dough into two equal-size balls, pat each ball into a 6-inch slightly mounded circle, and cut each circle into 8 wedges. To make rounds, roll the dough to 3/4 inch thick and cut with a floured 2-inch biscuit cutter. Place rounds at least an inch apart on an ungreased baking sheet and brush with egg white.

Bake 12–15 minutes or until golden. Serve warm with butter and jam. Makes 16 wedges or approximately 20 rounds.

BASIC BRITISH SCONES

This scone both looks good and has a nice taste for such inexpensive ingredients. (Supposedly cream of tartar as a leavening agent has a quick reaction time. Thus, mix, shape, and get these scones into the oven as swiftly as possible.)

2 cups all-purpose flour

¼ cup granulated sugar

1 tsp. cream of tartar

½ tsp. baking soda

⅛ tsp. salt

¼ cup margarine, chilled and cut into pieces

¾ cup milk

Preheat oven to 425 degrees Fahrenheit.

Combine dry ingredients in a medium-sized bowl. Add margarine and cut into the flour mixture with a pastry blender or two knives to make a coarse meal. Add milk and mix quickly, just until blended.

Turn the dough onto a floured board or cloth and knead lightly a few times. Roll to ¾-inch thick and cut with a floured 2-inch biscuit cutter. Place the rounds on an ungreased baking sheet (close together if you want soft sides, farther apart if you want crispy sides). If desired, sprinkle with sugar and press in slightly.

Bake 10–12 minutes or until golden. Serve warm with butter and the spread of your choice. Makes about 20–22 round scones.

CREAM SCONES

This light, flaky scone is absolutely scrumptious as long as you serve it warm with butter and jam.

2 cups all-purpose flour

2 tsp. baking powder

½ tsp. salt

¼ cup granulated sugar

½ cup unsalted butter, chilled
   and cut into pieces

¾ cup heavy whipping cream

1 large egg

¼ tsp. vanilla extract

Preheat oven to 400 degrees Fahrenheit.

Combine dry ingredients in a medium-sized bowl. Add the butter and cut into the flour mixture with a pastry blender or two knives to make a coarse meal. In a separate bowl combine the liquid ingredients and then add all at once to the dry ingredients. Mix just until blended.

Turn the dough out onto a floured surface and knead lightly a few times. Divide into two equal-sized balls. Pat each ball into a 6-inch circle, slightly mounded in shape. Cut each circle into 8 wedges and place on an ungreased baking sheet, allowing space between each wedge.

Bake 15 minutes or until golden brown. Makes 16 wedges.

PLAIN BUTTERMILK SCONES

This scone rises well and has a good shape and flavor. While not necessary, the sugar sprinkled on top adds a nice touch.

2 cups all-purpose flour

3 tbsp. granulated sugar

2 tsp. baking powder

½ tsp salt

⅓ cup margarine or unsalted butter, chilled and cut into pieces

1 large egg

½ cup buttermilk

Topping:

granulated sugar

Preheat oven to 400 degrees Fahrenheit.

Combine dry ingredients in a medium-sized bowl. Add butter or margarine and cut into the flour mixture with pastry blender or two knives to make a coarse meal. In a separate bowl blend the egg and buttermilk together with a small whisk or fork. Combine with dry ingredients and mix just until blended.

Turn the dough out onto a floured surface, knead lightly, and divide into two equal-sized balls. Pat each ball into a 6-inch circle, slightly mounded. With a floured knife, cut each circle into 8 wedges and place on an ungreased baking sheet, allowing space between each wedge, or roll dough out to ¾ inch thick and cut into 2-inch rounds with a floured biscuit cutter.

Sprinkle with granulated sugar and lightly pat the sugar into the surface of each scone.

Bake 10–12 minutes or until golden. Serve warm with butter and marmalade or jam. Makes 16 wedges or 20 two-inch rounds.

(Sometimes the scone dough seems a little difficult to mix together. Instead of stirring, use a flexible rubber spatula and a slicing motion to convince the wet and dry ingredients to blend decently. Flipping the mass of dough over in the bowl a couple of times during the slicing process picks up all the dry ingredients.)

SOUR CREAM CLOUD SCONES

This recipe makes puffy little scones, but you must mix, form, and get them into the oven quickly.

2 cups all-purpose flour

3 tbsp. granulated sugar

2 tsp. baking powder

½ tsp. baking soda

½ tsp. salt

½ cup unsalted butter, chilled
   and cut into pieces

¾ cup dairy sour cream

1 large egg

¼ tsp. vanilla extract

Glaze:

1 egg white, slightly beaten

Preheat oven to 400 degrees Fahrenheit.

Combine dry ingredients in a medium-sized bowl. Add the butter and cut into the flour mixture with pastry blender or two knives to make a coarse meal. In a separate bowl blend the sour cream, egg and vanilla extract together with a small whisk or fork. Combine with the dry ingredients and mix just until blended.

Turn the dough onto a floured surface, knead lightly, and divide into two equal-sized balls. Pat each ball into a 6-inch circle, slightly mounded. With a floured knife, cut each circle into 8 wedges and place on an ungreased baking sheet, allowing space between each scone. Or roll dough out to ¾ inch thick and cut into rounds with a floured 2-inch biscuit cutter.

Brush with the egg white, if desired. Bake 10 minutes or until a light golden brown. Makes 16 wedges or about 18–20 rounds.

SWEET BUTTERMILK SCONES

The vanilla and extra sugar makes this a sweet scone that tastes wonderful with sliced strawberries.

2 cups all-purpose flour

½ cup granulated sugar

1½ tsp. baking powder

½ tsp. baking soda

¼ tsp. salt

⅓ cup unsalted butter, chilled and cut into pieces

½ cup buttermilk

1 large egg

1½ tsp. vanilla extract

Preheat oven to 400 degrees Fahrenheit.

Combine dry ingredients in a medium-sized bowl. Add the butter and cut into the flour mixture with a pastry blender or two knives to make a coarse meal. In a separate bowl blend together the buttermilk, egg, and vanilla extract with a small whisk or fork. Combine with the dry ingredients and mix just until blended.

Turn the dough onto a floured board, knead lightly, and divide into two equal-sized balls. Pat each ball into a 6-inch circle, slightly mounded in shape. Cut each circle into 6 wedges and place on an ungreased baking sheet, allowing space between each scone.

Bake 12–15 minutes or until light brown. Makes 12 scones.

WASTE NOT, WANT NOT

One glorious, warm autumn my parents were hired to tend a small neighboring farm while its elderly owners made one last trip back East to visit relatives. My parents' duties were to care for a milk cow, an ancient retired plow horse with enormous feet, and about one hundred chickens.

Each day the eggs where to be collected, candled, and packed for the co-op. The cow needed to be milked twice a day and the milk put through the hand-crank separator, with a certain percentage of the milk and cream also going to the co-op. Any eggs not perfect and the remainder of the milk and cream, plus the remainder of a large garden and any fruit, could be used by our family any way we desired.

For my parents, who had survived part of the Great Depression by managing to pick just enough cotton each day to purchase enough beans for the next day's meals, this farm arrangement sounded as though it was sent from heaven.

The trees of the small apple orchard were dropping so many apples that my parents resorted to the use of an old cider press they found in one of the sheds. All the cream was churned into butter, wrapped, and stored in the "frozen food lockers" in the town's grocery store. They battled the hornets and bees for the fruit from a two-story pear tree next to the tall, skinny farmhouse.

Big tubs of apple and pear butter blurped on the stove, and then my mother turned her attention to the tail ends of the garden. She picked everything that was there, even the vegetables past their prime. Corn, beans, tomatoes, onions, and probably things I cannot remember all went through the food grinder and into the pressure canner. This concoction was the most wonderful soup base that a person could want, and there were so many quarts that we used it for years. My mother was not about to let all this good food escape her grasp.

You may think that all this work sounds like an excess of frugality. To my family it was simply being smart. We were being good stewards over the bounty of the land that was our temporary responsibility. No one knows what the future will bring, and often fate is kind and hands us a bonus. It is up to us to accept it or reject it. My mother chose to "make hay" while the sun shone.

Rosalie Clarke

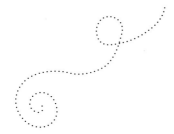

FRUIT AND NUT SCONES

I shall always be grateful for the times my mother sent the florist to my door and in his hands were hyacinths.

"If thou of fortune be bereft,
And in thy store there be but left
Two loaves—sell one, and with the dole
Buy hyacinths to feed thy soul."

—James Terry White
from the poem *Not by Bread Alone* (1907)

BUTTERMILK SCONES WITH CURRANTS

For this scone to be pretty and have the best taste, be sure to include the topping.

2 cups all-purpose flour

¼ cup granulated sugar

½ tsp. salt

1½ tsp. baking powder

½ tsp. baking soda

½ cup unsalted butter, chilled and cut into pieces

½ cup dried currants (or dried cranberries), coarsely chopped

⅔ cup buttermilk

2 tbsp. water

Topping:

1 tbsp. cream or milk

granulated sugar

Preheat oven to 400 degrees Fahrenheit.

Combine dry ingredients in a medium-sized bowl. Add the butter and cut into the flour mixture with a pastry blender or two knives to make a coarse meal. Add dried currants (or dried cranberries), and stir with a spoon until all the pieces of fruit are coated with flour.

In a separate bowl mix the buttermilk and water together with a fork or whisk. Combine the dry and wet ingredients, and stir with a wooden spoon or spatula just until blended.

Turn the dough out onto a floured surface, knead lightly, and divide into two equal-sized balls. Pat each ball into a 6½-inch circle, slightly mounded in shape. Cut each circle into 8 wedges and place on an ungreased baking sheet, allowing space between each wedge.

Brush scones with the cream or milk, and sprinkle with granulated sugar. Bake 12–15 minutes or until golden. Serve warm with butter and marmalade. Makes 16 wedges.

FRENCH APPLE~CREAM SCONES

"French" sounds elegant, doesn't it? Actually, the idea for this scone came from an old cookbook that belonged to my grandmother. The turbinado sugar provides sweetness and crunch. These are our daughters' favorite scones.

2 cups all-purpose flour

½ cup turbinado sugar

2 tsp. baking powder

1 tsp. cinnamon

½ tsp. salt

¼ tsp. nutmeg

½ cup unsalted butter, chilled
    and cut into pieces

¾ cup apple, peeled, cored, and
    diced into ¼-inch pieces

½ cup heavy whipping cream

1 tsp. vanilla extract

1 large egg, slightly beaten

Topping:

cinnamon and sugar

Preheat oven to 400 degrees Fahrenheit.

In a medium-sized bowl, combine the dry ingredients. Add the butter and cut into the flour mixture with pastry blender or two knives to make a coarse meal. Add the diced apple and stir with a spoon until the apple pieces are coated with the flour mixture and distributed evenly throughout.

In another bowl combine the cream, vanilla, and egg.

Add the wet ingredients to the dry ingredients and mix together gently, just until blended.

Turn the dough onto a floured surface, knead lightly, and divide into two equal-sized balls. Pat each ball into a 6-inch circle, slightly domed in shape. Cut each circle into 8 wedges and place on an ungreased baking sheet, allowing space between each scone. Sprinkle with cinnamon and sugar, if desired.

Bake 15–17 minutes or until golden brown. Makes 16 wedges.

ALL~THOSE~RAISINS SCONES

My husband loves raisins. When he saw me shaping these scones, his eyes lit up. "Look at all those raisins!" he exclaimed. He may have been happy, but I was having a hard time keeping "all those raisins" in the dough where they belonged. If you have a raisin lover in your home, by all means use a whole cup of raisins. If you want fewer raisins, cut back to ½ cup of raisins, and add one more tablespoon of granulated sugar.

2 cups all-purpose flour

2 tbsp. granulated sugar

2 tsp. baking powder

½ tsp. baking soda

½ tsp. salt

½ tsp. ground nutmeg

½ cup unsalted butter, chilled
    and cut into pieces

1 cup raisins

½ cup buttermilk

1 yolk of a large egg (save the egg
    white for the glaze)

¼ cup water (approximately)

Glaze:

1 egg white, slightly beaten

granulated sugar

Preheat oven to 375 degrees Fahrenheit.

Combine the dry ingredients in a medium-sized bowl. Add the butter and cut into the flour mixture with a pastry blender or two knives to make a coarse meal. Add the raisins and stir in with a spoon.

In a small measuring pitcher combine the buttermilk, egg yolk, and enough water to equal ¾ cup of total liquid. Add to the dry ingredients and mix together gently just until blended.

Turn the mixture onto a floured surface and knead gently a few times. Divide the dough in half and shape into two balls. Pat each ball into a 6-inch circle, slightly mounded. With a floured knife, cut each circle into 8 wedges.

On an ungreased baking sheet, arrange the wedges back into the two circles with the wedges ¼ inch from each other.

Brush with the egg white and sprinkle with granulated sugar, if desired.

Bake 16–18 minutes or until medium golden brown. Makes 16 scones.

GOLDEN LEMON~CREAM SCONES

Golden raisins add a nice flavor to this sweet scone.

2 cups all-purpose flour

1/3 cup granulated sugar

2 tsp. baking powder

1/2 tsp. baking soda

1/2 tsp. salt

1 tsp. lemon rind, finely grated

1/3 cup unsalted butter, chilled
   and cut into pieces

1/2 cup golden raisins

1/2 cup heavy whipping cream

1 large egg

1/4 tsp. vanilla extract

Preheat oven to 400 degrees Fahrenheit.

In a medium-sized bowl, stir together the flour, sugar, baking powder, baking soda, salt, and lemon rind. Add the butter and cut into the flour mixture with a pastry blender or two knives to make a coarse meal. Stir in the golden raisins.

In a separate bowl blend the cream, egg, and vanilla extract together with a small whisk or fork. Combine with the dry ingredients and mix just until blended. Add a little more cream, if needed.

Turn the dough onto a floured surface and knead gently five to six times.

For wedges, divide the dough in half, shape into two balls, and pat each ball into a 6-inch circle, slightly mounded. Cut each circle into 8 wedges.

For rounds: roll the dough out to ½-inch thick and cut into rounds with a floured 2-inch biscuit cutter. Place the scones on an ungreased baking sheet, allowing an inch or more between each scone.

Bake 10 minutes or until a light golden brown. Serve warm with butter or margarine, fresh fruit, and a favorite cheese. Makes 16 wedges or approximately 20 rounds.

BIT O' FRUIT AND NUTS SCONES

Versatile and delightful, this scone is great with the tea of your choice.

2 cups all-purpose flour

½ cup granulated sugar

1½ tsp. baking powder

½ tsp. baking soda

¼ tsp. salt

½ cup unsalted butter, chilled
   and cut into pieces

½ cup dried fruit (raisins, dates,
   cranberries), chopped

¼ cup walnuts, chopped

1 tsp. vanilla extract

1 large egg

½ cup buttermilk
   (approximately)

Preheat oven to 400 degrees Fahrenheit.

Combine dry ingredients in a medium-sized bowl. Add the butter and cut into the flour mixture with pastry blender or two knives to make a coarse meal. Add the dried fruit and walnuts and stir with a spoon until all the fruit and nuts are coated with the flour mixture.

In a small measuring pitcher put the vanilla extract, egg, and add enough buttermilk to equal ¾ cup liquid total. Blend together with a whisk or fork.

Combine the dry and wet ingredients and mix together just until blended. *(You may have to knead the dough in the bowl a bit, turning the dough completely over a couple of times to incorporate all the dry pieces.)*

Turn the dough onto a floured surface, knead lightly, and divide into two equal-sized balls. Pat each ball into a 6-inch circle and cut each circle into 6 or 8 wedges. On an ungreased baking sheet, arrange the wedges back into the two circles with the wedges ¼ inch from each other. This helps the scones bake up instead of out and maintain a neat scone appearance.

Bake 10–12 minutes or until golden brown. Serve warm with Mock Devonshire Cream (page 76) or Lemon Curd (page 77). Makes 12–16 wedges.

MAPLE~WALNUT SCONES

These scones are not only delicious served warm out of the oven, but they also taste wonderful later if reheated for a few seconds in the microwave. Our oldest son was perfectly willing to taste test this recipe over and over.

2 cups all-purpose flour

3 tbsp. brown sugar, packed

2 tsp. baking powder

¼ tsp .salt

½ cup unsalted butter or
    margarine, chilled and cut
    into pieces

½ cup walnuts, coarsely chopped

⅓ cup maple syrup

1 large egg

milk

Topping:

2 tbsp. brown sugar, packed

2 tbsp. finely chopped walnuts

Preheat oven to 400 degrees Fahrenheit.

In a small bowl mix the ingredients for the topping and set aside.

Combine the flour, brown sugar, baking powder, and salt in a medium-sized bowl. Add the butter or margarine and cut into the flour mixture with a pastry blender or two knives to make a coarse meal. Stir in the chopped walnuts.

In a small measuring pitcher combine the maple syrup, egg, and enough milk to equal ¾ cup total liquid ingredients. Combine the wet and dry ingredients, and mix just until blended.

Turn the dough onto a floured surface and knead lightly five to six times. Divide the dough in half and shape into two balls. Pat each ball into a 6½-inch circle, slightly mounded. Place both circles on an ungreased baking sheet and, using a wet hand, slightly pat the tops of each circle.

Sprinkle each circle with the topping and press in lightly so it sticks. With a floured knife, carefully cut each circle into 8 wedges, wiggling the knife from side to side to make a small space between each scone.

Bake 15 minutes or until golden. Immediately remove from the cookie sheet, being careful when separating the wedges. Makes 16 scones.

DATE SCONES

This is a beautiful scone that is absolutely delicious served with sliced apple and cheddar cheese. Be sure to brush the tops with the egg white so that they will have a lovely golden brown color.

2 cups all-purpose flour

¼ cup brown sugar, packed

2 tsp. baking powder

¼ tsp. salt

⅓ cup margarine, chilled and cut
   into pieces

½ cup pitted dates, cut into
   ¼-inch pieces

1 egg yoke (save white for glaze)

3 tbsp. maple syrup

½ cup milk

Glaze:

1 egg white, slightly beaten

Preheat oven to 400 degrees Fahrenheit.

Combine the dry ingredients in a medium-sized bowl. Add the margarine and cut into the flour mixture with a pastry blender or two knives to make a coarse meal. Stir in the dates, making sure that the pieces are evenly distributed throughout the flour mixture. You might have to use your fingers to separate any date pieces that insist on sticking together.

In another small bowl combine the egg yoke, milk, and maple syrup, and whip with a fork. Add the liquid ingredients to the dry ingredients and mix quickly, just until blended.

Turn the mixture onto a floured surface and knead gently a few times. Divide the dough in half, shape into two balls, and pat each ball into a 6-inch circle, slightly mounded. Using a floured knife, cut each circle into 8 wedges. On an ungreased baking sheet, loosely arrange the wedges back into the two 6-inch circles, leaving ¼-inch space between each wedge. This will ensure a straighter, softer side on the scones.

Brush scone tops with the egg white.

Bake 15–17 minutes or until golden brown. Makes 16 wedges.

ORANGE~RAISIN SCONES

With orange to give it a bit of tang, raisins to give it a bit of sweet, and cinnamon and sugar to give it a nice crunchy top, what's not to like about this scone?

2 cups all-purpose flour

¼ cup granulated sugar

1½ tsp. baking powder

½ tsp. baking soda

½ tsp. salt

1 tsp. freshly grated orange rind

½ cup unsalted butter, chilled
   and cut into pieces

½ cup raisins

¾ cup buttermilk

Topping:

2 tbsp. granulated sugar

¼ tsp. cinnamon

Preheat oven to 375 degrees Fahrenheit.

Mix the ingredients for the topping in a small bowl and set aside.

Combine the first six ingredients in a medium-sized bowl. Add butter and cut into flour mixture with pastry blender or two knives to make a coarse meal. Add the raisins and stir with a spoon.

Add the buttermilk to the dry ingredients and mix together gently just until blended.

Turn the dough onto a floured surface, knead briefly and roll to ¾-inch thick. Cut into 2-inch rounds with a floured biscuit cutter and place on an ungreased baking sheet. Sprinkle with the cinnamon and sugar topping and pat in gently.

Bake 12 minutes or until light golden brown. Makes about 20 round scones. Serve with Mock Devonshire Cream (page 76).

APPLE SCONES WITH WHOLE WHEAT AND CINNAMON

These scones will make your kitchen smell spicy-warm on a cold winter morning. Be sure to brush with egg white for a shiny finish.

1½ cups all-purpose flour

½ cup whole wheat flour

¼ cup granulated sugar

2¾ tsp. baking powder

½ tsp. cinnamon

½ tsp. salt

¼ tsp. baking soda

4 tbsp. unsalted butter, chilled
   and cut into pieces

1 cup apple, peeled, cored, and
   diced

1 large egg

½ cup buttermilk

Glaze:

egg white, slightly beaten

Preheat oven to 400 degrees Fahrenheit.

Combine dry ingredients in a medium-sized bowl. Add the butter and cut into the flour mixture with a pastry blender or two knives to make a coarse meal. Add the diced apple and stir with a spoon until all the apple pieces are coated with the flour mixture.

In a separate bowl blend the egg and the buttermilk together with a whisk or fork.

Combine the dry and wet ingredients, and mix them together just until blended. Use a rubber spatula to slice into and turn the ingredients.

Turn the dough onto a floured board, knead lightly, roll dough ½ to ¾-inch thick and cut into rounds with a floured 2-inch biscuit cutter, carefully kneading and rerolling the scraps as necessary. Put on an ungreased baking sheet about an inch apart and brush with the slightly beaten egg white.

Bake 10–12 minutes or until golden. They're wonderful with butter or margarine. Makes 15–18 rounds.

CHERRY-ALMOND SCONES

This is a lovely scone for breakfast or brunch—sweet and beautiful.

2 cups all-purpose flour

½ cup granulated sugar

2 tsp. baking powder

½ tsp. baking soda

½ tsp. salt

½ cup unsalted butter, chilled
and cut into pieces

¾ cup dried cherries, chopped

½ cup buttermilk

1 large egg

¼ tsp. almond extract

Topping:

1 egg white, slightly beaten

sliced almonds

Preheat oven to 400 degrees Fahrenheit.

In a medium-sized bowl, stir together the flour, sugar, baking powder, baking soda, and salt. Add the butter and cut into the flour mixture with pastry blender or two knives to make a coarse meal. Stir in the dried cherries until each piece is coated with the flour mixture.

In a separate bowl blend the buttermilk, egg, and almond extract together with a small whisk or fork. Combine with the dry ingredients and mix just until blended.

Turn the dough onto a floured board and knead gently five to six times. Divide the dough in half, shape into two balls, and pat each ball into a 6-inch circle, slightly mounded. Using a floured knife, cut each circle into 8 wedges. On an ungreased baking sheet, loosely arrange wedges back into the two circles, leaving ¼-inch space between each wedge. This will ensure a straighter, softer side on the scones.

Brush tops of the scones with egg white, and decorate with sliced almonds.

Bake 12–14 minutes or until golden brown. Makes 16 wedges.

GOLDEN RAISIN SCONES

This is a delicious scone with a warm, golden flavor and a sparkling top.

2 cups all-purpose flour

1/3 cup turbinado sugar

2 tsp. baking powder

1/4 tsp. baking soda

1/2 tsp. salt

2 tsp. freshly grated orange rind

1/2 cup unsalted butter, chilled and
   cut into pieces

1/2 cup golden raisins

1/2 cup buttermilk

1 large egg

Glaze:

 1 egg white, slightly beaten

Topping:

1 tbsp. turbinado sugar

1 tbsp. finely chopped walnuts or
   pecans

Preheat oven to 375 degrees Fahrenheit.

Mix together topping ingredients in a small bowl and set aside.

Combine the dry ingredients and the orange rind in a medium-sized bowl. Cut in the butter with two knives or a pastry cutter to make a coarse meal. Stir in the golden raisins until all the raisins are coated with the flour mixture, using your fingers to separate the raisins from each other, if necessary.

In a separate bowl whisk the buttermilk and egg together until smooth. Add the liquid ingredients to the dry ingredients and mix with a wooden spoon or rubber spatula just until blended.

Turn the dough onto a floured surface and knead lightly five to six times. Divide the dough in half and knead each half a few times. Shape each half into a ball and pat into a 6-inch circle, slightly mounded. With a floured knife, cut each circle into 8 wedges. Place

the wedges on an ungreased baking sheet about an inch apart. Brush with egg white, sprinkle with topping, and gently pat in so it sticks to the top of the scone.

Bake 15–20 minutes or until golden brown. Makes 16 wedges.

CRANBERRY SCONES

This is a nice recipe that still tastes good the next day. Just zap one of the scones in the microwave for 8-10 seconds and, as our sons say, "You're good to go."

2½ cups all-purpose flour

½ cup granulated sugar

2½ tsp. baking powder

½ tsp. baking soda

½ tsp. salt

¼ cup unsalted butter or margarine, chilled and cut into pieces

1 cup raw cranberries, coarsely chopped

2 tsp. fresh orange rind, finely grated

½ cup buttermilk

¼ cup water

Topping:

granulated sugar

Preheat oven to 400 degrees Fahrenheit.

Combine the dry ingredients in a medium-sized bowl. Add the butter or margarine and cut into the flour mixture with pastry blender or two knives to make a coarse meal. Add the chopped cranberries and the orange rind, and stir with a spoon until the cranberries are coated with the flour mixture and the orange rind is evenly distributed throughout.

In another bowl combine the buttermilk and water. Add the wet ingredients to the dry ingredients and mix together gently, just until blended.

Turn the dough onto a floured surface, knead lightly, and divide into two equal-sized balls. Pat each ball into a 6-inch circle, slightly domed in shape. Cut each circle into 8 wedges and place on an ungreased baking sheet, allowing space between each scone. Sprinkle the tops with granulated sugar and pat in gently.

Bake 12 minutes or until lightly browned. Makes 16 wedges. Serve with butter and Mock Devonshire Cream (page 76).

ORANGE~POPPYSEED SCONES

This is a nice scone with a hint of orange and a satisfying crunch—delicious with butter or margarine.

2¼ cups all-purpose flour

½ cup granulated sugar

¼ cup poppy seeds

1 tsp. cream of tartar

¼ tsp. baking soda

½ tsp. salt

1 tsp. freshly grated orange rind

½ cup unsalted butter, chilled
and cut into pieces

⅓ cup buttermilk

1 large egg

¼ cup orange juice

½ tsp. vanilla extract

Preheat oven to 375 degrees Fahrenheit.

Combine the first seven ingredients in a medium-sized mixing bowl.

Cut in the butter with two knives or a pastry cutter to make a coarse meal. In a separate bowl combine the buttermilk, egg, orange juice, and vanilla extract with a whisk until smooth.

Add the liquid ingredients to the dry ingredients and mix with a rubber spatula or wooden spoon just until blended. Turn the dough onto a floured surface and knead lightly five to six times. Roll the dough out to ¾ inch thick and cut into rounds with a floured 2-inch biscuit cutter.

Bake 12–15 minutes or until golden brown. Makes 20–22 rounds. Try with orange marmalade and Mock Devonshire Cream (page 76).

APRICOT-GINGER SCONES

Try this not-too-sweet scone with the tea of your choice.

2 cups all-purpose flour

3 tbsp. granulated sugar

2 tsp. baking powder

½ tsp. baking soda

½ tsp. salt

½ tsp. fresh lemon rind, finely
   grated

½ cup unsalted butter, chilled
   and cut into pieces

½ cup dried apricots, chopped

2 tbsp. crystallized ginger,
   minced

½ cup buttermilk

1 large egg

¼ tsp. vanilla extract

Glaze:

1 egg white, slightly beaten

Preheat oven to 400 degrees Fahrenheit.

In a medium-sized bowl stir together the dry ingredients. Add the lemon rind and stir until evenly distributed. Add the butter and cut into the flour mixture with a pastry blender or two knives to make a coarse meal. Stir in the dried apricots and crystallized ginger.

In a separate bowl blend the buttermilk, egg, and vanilla extract together with a small whisk or fork. Add the liquid to the dry ingredients and mix together gently, just until blended.

Turn the dough out onto a floured surface and knead five to six times. Divide into two balls, and form each into a 6-inch circle, slightly mounded. Cut each circle into 8 wedges, or roll the dough out to ¾-inch thick and cut into 2-inch rounds. Place scones an inch or so apart on an ungreased baking sheet. Brush with egg white, if desired.

Bake 10 minutes or until golden. Serve warm with butter or margarine. Makes 16 wedges or approximately 20 rounds.

GiNGERED PECAN SCONES

For a unique flavor and a beautiful presentation, carefully cut each warm scone in half and put whipped cream and sliced strawberries between the two layers. They're wonderful!

2 cups all-purpose flour

1 tbsp. baking powder

2 tbsp. granulated sugar

½ tsp. salt

½ cup unsalted butter, chilled and cut into pieces

¼ cup crystallized ginger, chopped

½ cup pecans, chopped

⅓ cup heavy whipping cream

1 large egg, slightly beaten

Preheat oven to 375 degrees Fahrenheit.

Combine dry ingredients in a medium-sized bowl. Add the butter and cut into the flour mixture with two knives or a pastry cutter until mixture resembles a coarse meal. Stir in the chopped ginger and pecans.

In another bowl briefly blend the whipping cream and egg together with a wire whisk. Add liquid ingredients to dry ingredients. Stir in quickly but lightly with a wooden spoon or a rubber spatula.

Turn the dough onto a floured surface and knead five to six times. Divide into two balls and form each into a 6-inch circle, slightly mounded. Cut each circle into 8 wedges, or roll the dough out to ¾-inch thick and cut into 2-inch rounds. Place scones an inch or so apart on an ungreased baking sheet.

Bake for 15 minutes or until a light brown. Makes 16 wedges or about 20 rounds.

ALMOND~POPPYSEED SCONES

Choose this recipe when you need a scone with a light, sweet flavor and an elegant look.
It's sure to impress your guests.

2 cups all-purpose flour

1/3 cup granulated sugar

1 tbsp. poppy seeds

2 tsp. baking powder

1/2 tsp. salt

1/2 cup unsalted butter, chilled
   and cut into pieces

1/3 cup sour cream

1 large egg

1 large egg yolk (reserve the egg
   white for the glaze)

1 tsp. almond extract

2 tbsp. milk (approximately)

Glaze:

egg white from large egg

sliced almonds

Preheat oven to 400 degrees Fahrenheit.

Combine dry ingredients in a medium-sized bowl. Cut in the butter with two knives or a pastry cutter to make a coarse meal. In a small measuring pitcher combine the sour cream, whole egg, egg yolk, almond extract, and enough milk to make 3/4 cup total liquid ingredients.

Add the liquid ingredients to the dry ingredients and mix with a rubber spatula or wooden spoon just until blended. (A slicing and turning motion seems to work best.) Turn dough onto a floured surface and knead lightly five to six times.

For wedges: divide the dough into two equal-sized balls. Pat each ball into a 6-inch circle, slightly domed in shape. Cut each circle into 8 wedges.

For rounds: roll dough out to ½-inch thick and cut into rounds with a floured 2-inch biscuit cutter.

Place wedges or rounds on an ungreased baking sheet, allowing an inch or more between each scone. Brush with egg white and decorate tops with sliced almonds. Carefully brush a little more egg white on top of each scone to help hold the almonds in place.

Bake 12 minutes or until golden brown. Makes 16 wedges or about 20 rounds.

HAZELNUT~RASPBERRY SCONES

Can you say "gourmet"? Have your hot chocolate ready. These scones are sooo good!

2 cups all-purpose flour

1/3 cup granulated sugar

2 tsp. baking powder

1/2 tsp. baking soda

1/2 tsp. salt

1/2 cup hazelnuts, peeled, toasted, and finely ground (see page 75)

1/2 cup unsalted butter, chilled and cut into pieces

1/2 cup buttermilk

1/4 cup water

4 tbsp. raspberry preserves, divided

Glaze:

1 egg white, slightly beaten

Preheat oven to 400 degrees Fahrenheit.

Combine the dry ingredients and the ground hazelnuts in a medium-sized bowl. Add the butter and cut into the flour mixture with a pastry blender or two knives to make a coarse meal.

In a separate bowl mix together the buttermilk and water. Combine the liquid ingredients with the dry ingredients and mix with a spoon or rubber spatula just until blended. Turn the mixture onto floured surface and knead gently a few times. Divide the dough into four equal pieces and shape each piece into a ball. Pat each ball into a 6-inch circle, slightly mounded.

Spread raspberry preserves evenly over two of the circles, leaving a 1/2-inch plain border. Invert a plain circle over each of the preserve-covered circles and press edges together slightly to seal.

Place both filled circles on an ungreased baking sheet.

Using a floured knife, cut each circle into 8 wedges and separate the wedges approximately ¼ inch. The wedges must remain in a circle to keep the layers of dough from sliding apart across the preserves during baking.

Brush the wedges with egg white and bake 14–16 minutes or until golden brown. Makes 16 wedges.

WALNUT~BLACKBERRY SCONES

This is a scone to remind you of the harvest season. Give these as a gift with a jar of your favorite blackberry preserves.

2 cups all-purpose flour

1/3 cup granulated sugar

2 tsp. baking powder

1/2 tsp. baking soda

1/2 tsp. salt

1/2 tsp. fresh orange rind, finely grated

1/2 cup walnuts, finely chopped

1/2 cup unsalted butter, chilled and cut into pieces

1/2 cup buttermilk

1/4 cup water

4 tbsp. blackberry preserves, divided

Glaze:

1 egg white, slightly beaten

Preheat oven to 400 degrees Fahrenheit.

Combine dry ingredients, orange rind, and chopped walnuts in a medium-sized bowl. Add the butter and cut into the flour mixture with a pastry blender or two knives to make a coarse meal. In a separate bowl mix together the buttermilk and water.

Combine liquid ingredients with the dry ingredients and mix with spoon or rubber spatula just until blended. Turn the mixture onto a floured surface and knead gently a few times. Divide dough into four equal pieces and shape each piece into a 6-inch circle, slightly mounded. Spread blackberry preserves evenly over two of the circles, leaving a ½-inch plain border. Invert a plain circle over each of the preserve-covered circles and press edges together slightly to seal.

Place the two filled circles on an ungreased baking sheet. Using a floured knife, cut each circle into 8 wedges and separate the wedges approximately ¼ inch. The wedges must remain in a circle to keep the layers of dough from sliding apart across the preserves during baking.

Brush the wedges with egg white and bake 14–16 minutes or until golden brown. Makes 16 wedges.

CULTURAL THINGS

My father died suddenly and unexpectedly when I was twelve and my sister was seven. My mother was left to provide for her family by housecleaning and ironing for more fortunate women in our community and by working as a cook at the school and washing dishes at a restaurant. She was used to working hard ever since she finished the eighth grade, but this must have been a terrible burden for her, knowing that she had the sole responsibility for the three of us.

Despite lack of funds, my mother was determined that we would not lead lives of cultural poverty, and so our lives were filled with trips to the library, after which we would return with armloads of books and records. She loved to read to us, and every evening we would enjoy another chapter or two after we had demonstrated that we had absorbed the previous night's reading. We wallowed in Kipling and Walter Farley, plus books from Mom's childhood such as *Queen Maji's Little People* and *The Water Babies*. Edgar Rice Burroughs was a favorite, and I think that my mother was trying to relive her own childhood with those books as she told how she and her sister, Mildred, would make siphoning straws out of dandelion stems and read *Tarzan* in the heat of Minnesota summers while filling up on water through those unique contraptions. The borrowed records opened the world of classical music, sea shanties, and South Africa's precious Miriam Makeba. Mom made sure that we memorized the words to all of the patriotic songs, and to this day I have the same reaction on hearing them as did my mother. World War II had taken its toll, and as memories would rush to the surface, she would cry.

Our mother managed to set aside a bit of money every month so that when stage productions came to the city near us, there was money for tickets. We attended *The Passion Play* (the original, from Germany), and when Christ died on the cross, the building actually shook. When we emerged, we found that there had been a real earthquake at that exact moment.

We saw the ballet—from way up in the top of the balcony, of course—taking turns to look at the elaborate makeup with little opera glasses that my mom had found at some yard sale. (I even wore a fancy black velvet cape that was a leftover from better times, making me feel quite elegant.) Every time Jose Greco and his Spanish dance troupe came to town, we had tickets. And we had several seasons of tickets for World Cavalcade, which was a traveling slide show narrated by the adventurous people who had taken the pictures. All of these things we experienced despite the poverty. I never knew one person in my school enjoying better circumstances who ever attended any of these cultural events. I will be forever grateful for the choices my mother made with her limited resources.

Rosalie Clarke

SWEET SCONES

He who knows not and knows that he knows
not, is simple—teach him.
He who knows and knows not that he knows is
asleep—wake him.
He who knows not and knows not that he
knows not is a fool—shun him.
But he who knows and knows that he knows is
wise—follow him.

—Quote found tucked inside Grandma's old
wooden recipe box and written in her hand

STREUSEL SCONES

These scones remind me of the coffee cakes I used to make for my brothers years ago.

2 cups all-purpose flour

¼ cup granulated sugar

2 tsp. baking powder

¼ tsp. baking soda

¼ tsp. salt

¼ cup margarine, chilled and
   cut into pieces

½ cup buttermilk

¼ cup water

Topping:

¼ cup quick-cooking oats

¼ cup brown sugar, packed

1 tbsp. margarine, melted

1 tbsp. all-purpose flour

½ tsp. ground cinnamon

Preheat oven to 400 degrees Fahrenheit.

Combine the first five ingredients in a medium-sized bowl. Add the margarine and cut it into the flour mixture with a pastry blender or two knives to make a coarse meal.

In another bowl combine the buttermilk and water. Add the wet ingredients to the dry ingredients and mix together gently, just until blended.

Turn the dough onto a floured surface, knead a few times, and divide into two equal-sized balls. Pat each ball into a 6-inch circle, slightly mounded, and place on an ungreased baking sheet.

In a small bowl mix together the ingredients for the topping until crumbly. Spread the topping over the top of the two 6-inch circles and gently pat in.

With a floured knife, cut each 6-inch circle into 8 wedges, wiggling the knife slightly to separate the wedges from each other. When the scones are done, you will be able to easily pull them apart. The sides will be straight and soft.

Bake 15 minutes or until golden brown. Makes 16 wedges.

CHOCOLATE MUMBLE SCONES

When I told our sons I needed them to do some more taste testing, they dutifully trudged up the stairs into the kitchen and took a bite of my latest experiment. Immediately their heads began nodding; they mumbled something to me and reached for the milk. I assumed that meant the recipe was okay.

2 cups all-purpose flour

½ cup + 1 tbsp. granulated sugar

⅓ cup unsweetened cocoa powder

2 tsp. baking powder

½ tsp. cinnamon

¼ tsp. salt

½ cup unsalted butter, chilled and
cut into pieces

¾ cup real semi-sweet chocolate
chips

½ cup sweetened, flaked coconut

½ cup heavy whipping cream

1 large egg, slightly beaten

1 tbsp. water

¼ tsp. vanilla extract

Topping:

1 egg white, slightly beaten

sweetened, flaked coconut

Preheat oven to 400 degrees Fahrenheit.

In a large bowl combine the first six ingredients. Add the butter and cut into the flour mixture with a pastry blender or two knives to make a coarse meal. Add the chocolate chips and the coconut and stir with a spoon until the chips and coconut are coated with the flour mixture and are evenly distributed throughout.

In another bowl combine the cream, egg, water, and vanilla extract. Add the wet ingredients to the dry ingredients and mix together. *(The dough will be stiff. I use a flat wooden spoon to cut and turn the ingredients until just blended.)*

Turn dough onto a floured surface, knead briefly, and roll out to ½ inch thick. Cut into 2-inch rounds with a floured biscuit cutter. Place an inch apart on an ungreased baking sheet.

Brush the surface of the scones with egg white, top with the flaked coconut, and press it in gently.

Bake 12–14 minutes, being careful that the coconut does not burn. Makes 20–22 rounds.

CHOCOLATE~CHOCOLATE SCONES

The moment I tasted this recipe I knew I had something good. These scones for chocolate lovers get eaten as quickly as I can make them.

2 cups all-purpose flour

½ cup + 1 tbsp. granulated sugar

⅓ cup unsweetened cocoa powder

2 tsp. baking powder

¼ tsp. salt

½ cup unsalted butter, chilled and cut into pieces

¾ cup real semi-sweet chocolate chips

½ cup walnuts, coarsely chopped

½ cup buttermilk

2 large eggs

Preheat oven to 375 degrees Fahrenheit.

In a medium-sized bowl carefully stir the dry ingredients together. (*Cocoa powder tends to fly out of the bowl if you stir too fast.*) Cut in the butter using a pastry cutter or two knives to make a coarse meal. Add the chocolate chips and chopped walnuts and mix until distributed evenly.

In a separate bowl or small measuring pitcher, blend the buttermilk and eggs with a fork or small whisk. Combine the liquid ingredients with the dry ingredients, and mix with a spoon or rubber spatula just until blended.

Turn the mixture onto a floured surface and knead gently a few times. Divide the dough in half, shape into two balls, and pat each ball into a 6-inch circle, slightly mounded. Using a floured knife, cut each circle into 8 wedges and place an inch or more apart on an ungreased baking sheet. Bake 15–17 minutes. Makes 16 wedges.

DOUBLE CHOCOLATE~HAZELNUT SCONES WITH RASPBERRY FILLING

This is definitely a decadent dessert scone. The women in our family practically swooned at the first bite.

2 cups all-purpose flour

½ cup granulated sugar

⅓ cup unsweetened cocoa powder

2 tsp. baking powder

½ tsp. salt

½ cup unsalted butter, chilled and cut into pieces

⅔ cup real semi-sweet chocolate chips

½ cup hazelnuts, skinned, toasted, and coarsely chopped (see page 75)

1 cup heavy whipping cream

1 large egg

½ tsp. vanilla extract

4 tbsp. raspberry preserves, divided

Topping:

2 tbsp. white chocolate chips, finely ground

Preheat oven to 400 degrees Fahrenheit.

In a medium-sized bowl combine the flour, sugar, cocoa, baking powder, and the salt. Add the butter and cut in with a pastry cutter or two knives to make a coarse meal. Stir in the chocolate chips and hazelnuts.

In another bowl combine the whipping cream, egg, and vanilla extract with a fork or small whisk. Pour the liquid ingredients in with the dry ingredients and mix with a flat wooden spoon until blended. The dough will be slightly stiff.

Turn the dough onto a floured surface, and knead five to six times. Divide the dough into four equal pieces, and shape each piece into a ball. Pat each ball into a 6-inch circle, slightly mounded. Spread raspberry preserves evenly over two of the circles, leaving a ½-inch border plain. Invert a plain circle over each of the preserve-covered circles, and press the edges together to seal.

Place the two filled circles on an ungreased baking sheet. Using a floured knife, cut each circle into six or eight wedges and separate the wedges by approximately ¼ inch. The wedges must remain in a circle to prevent the layers of dough from sliding apart across the preserves during baking.

Bake 15 minutes or until firm. Remove the scones from the oven, and transfer to a wire cooling rack. Dust immediately with finely ground white chocolate chips.

Let cool 10–15 minutes before serving. Makes 12 or 16 wedges.

GiNGERED SCONES

The crystallized ginger on the top of these scones is the perfect touch. Be sure to use it!

2 cups all-purpose flour

¼ cup granulated sugar

2 tsp. baking powder

¼ tsp. baking soda

½ tsp. salt

1 tsp. ground ginger

1 tsp. ground cinnamon

½ cup unsalted butter, chilled
   and cut into pieces

⅓ cup molasses

1 large egg, slightly beaten

⅓ cup milk (approximately)

Topping:

2 tbsp. crystallized ginger, finely
   chopped

1 tbsp. granulated sugar

Preheat oven to 400 degrees Fahrenheit.

For the topping: mix the crystallized ginger and granulated sugar in a blender on high speed; then set aside.

Combine the first seven ingredients in a medium-sized bowl. Add the butter and cut into the flour mixture with a pastry blender or two knives to make a coarse meal.

In a small measuring pitcher, combine molasses, egg, and enough milk to equal ¾ cup total liquid. Mix with a small whisk or a fork.

Combine liquid ingredients with the dry ingredients and mix with a spoon or rubber spatula just until blended. Turn the mixture onto a floured surface and knead gently a few times. Divide the dough in half and shape into two balls. Pat each ball into a 6-inch circle, slightly mounded. Moisten the palm of your hand with water, and lightly dampen each circle.

Sprinkle the topping over the dampened circles and gently press in. With a floured knife, cut each circle into 8 wedges. Reassemble the circles onto an ungreased baking sheet, leaving a small amount of space between each wedge

Bake 12 minutes. Makes 16 wedges. Try with Mock Devonshire Cream (page 76) and a jam of your choice.

APRICOT-WALNUT SCONES
WITH WHITE CHOCOLATE CHIPS

In this recipe, tangy apricot, crunchy walnut, and smooth white chocolate come together to make an interesting scone. While you can do this recipe in 2-inch rounds, it looks more imposing as a wedge.

2 cups all-purpose flour

1/3 cup granulated sugar

2 tsp. baking powder

1/2 tsp. salt

1/4 cup unsalted butter, chilled
and cut into pieces

1/3 cup dried apricots, cut into
very small pieces

1/3 cup walnuts, chopped

1/4 cup white chocolate chips

1/2 cup buttermilk

1 large egg

1 tsp. vanilla extract

Glaze:

egg white, slightly beaten

Preheat oven to 375 degrees Fahrenheit.

Combine the flour, sugar, baking powder, and salt in a medium-sized bowl. Add the butter and cut into the flour mixture with a pastry blender or two knives to make a coarse meal.

In a small bowl stir together the apricots, walnuts, and white chocolate chips. Add to the flour mixture, stir until evenly distributed and all the pieces are coated with the flour.

In a separate bowl blend together the buttermilk, egg, and vanilla extract with a small whisk or fork. Pour the wet ingredients into the dry ingredients, and mix together (a turning, slicing motion works well) until blended.

Turn the dough onto a floured surface, knead lightly, and divide into two equal-sized balls. Pat each ball into a 6-inch circle, slightly domed in shape. With a floured knife, cut each circle into 8 wedges and place on an ungreased baking sheet, allowing space between each scone.

Brush each scone with the slightly beaten egg white for a shiny brown finish. Bake 15 minutes or until golden brown. Serve warm. Makes 16 wedges.

GINGERBREAD~OAT SCONES

This is a hearty-looking scone that holds its shape well and tastes great with milk.

1¾ cups all-purpose flour

¾ cup quick-cooking oats

¼ cup granulated sugar

2 tsp. baking powder

½ tsp. baking soda

¼ tsp. salt

1 tsp. ground cinnamon

½ tsp. ground ginger

¼ tsp. ground cloves

½ cup unsalted butter, chilled
   and cut into pieces

½ cup buttermilk

¼ cup molasses

Topping:

1 egg white, slightly beaten

granulated sugar

Preheat oven to 400 degrees Fahrenheit.

Combine dry ingredients in a medium-sized bowl. Add the butter and cut into the flour mixture with a pastry blender or two knives to make a coarse meal.

In a separate bowl combine the buttermilk and molasses. Add the liquid ingredients to the dry ingredients and mix together gently, just until blended.

Turn the mixture onto a floured surface and knead lightly a few times. Divide the dough in half and shape into two balls. Pat each ball into a 6-inch circle, slightly mounded. With a floured knife, cut each circle into 8 wedges.

Arrange the wedges on an ungreased baking sheet at least an inch apart. Brush with egg white and sprinkle with granulated sugar, if desired.

Bake 12–15 minutes or until firm. Remove from the baking sheet and cool on a wire rack. Makes 16 scones. Try with Lemon Curd (page 77) or Mock Devonshire Cream (page 76).

WHITE CHOCOLATE~CHERRY OAT SCONES

The tartness of dried cherries combines with the smooth sweetness of white chocolate in this slightly chewy scone.

1¾ cups all-purpose flour

¼ cup whole wheat flour

¼ cup granulated sugar

2 tsp. baking powder

½ tsp. baking soda

½ tsp. salt

½ cup unsalted butter, chilled and cut into pieces

¾ cup quick-cooking oats

½ cup dried cherries, coarsely chopped

½ cup white chocolate chips

½ cup buttermilk

¼ cup water

1 large egg

Preheat oven to 375 degrees Fahrenheit.

Combine the first six ingredients in a medium-sized bowl. Cut in the butter with two knives or a pastry cutter to make a coarse meal. Stir in the oats, white chocolate chips, and cherries.

In a separate bowl combine the buttermilk, water, and egg with a whisk or fork. Add the liquid ingredients to the dry ingredients and mix just until blended.

Turn the dough onto a floured surface and knead lightly three to four times. Roll out to ¾-inch thick and cut into rounds with a floured 2-inch biscuit cutter. Place on an ungreased baking sheet, allowing an inch or more between each scone.

Bake 15 minutes or until golden brown. Makes about 20 rounds.

THE KITCHEN DRAWER

When I was still living at home, I never thought much about the items in the kitchen utensil drawer. They had just always been there, used mainly by my mother. We helped Mom in the kitchen, but she allowed my sister and me to be children as long as possible . . . before we would be required to face the responsibilities of adulthood and homes of our own.

That ignorance of the wonderful utility of various objects changed abruptly when I married. Almost the first thing that my mother did was set me down and explain to me the "facts" of the residents of that kitchen draw—primarily the heavy broad-backed Old Hickory brand butcher knife and the all-purpose kitchen shears. These two items are noted for their must-have versatility. As Mom handed me my own knife and shears, she let me know that no kitchen could long function easily without these items.

The shears do everything from cracking walnuts and loosening lids to cutting chicken bones. The knife has a broad back that allows it to be hit with a hammer without damage so it can be driven through steak bones and myriad other things. Its usefulness is limited only by the imagination of the cook. How else can you cut in half an acorn squash or even begin to tackle a watermelon?

Although forty-five years have passed, my mind still returns to that educational day whenever I whack the old knife through a stubborn item or cut chicken bones with the shears, and I cannot help but wonder what other, less-fortunate daughters use for these chores.

Rosalie Clarke

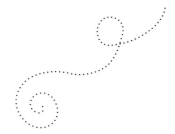

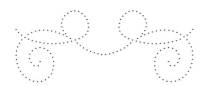

AND MORE

Reality is no further than an honest
conversation with your mother.

—Rosalie Clarke

SKINNING HAZELNUTS

This is the easiest technique I've tried for skinning hazelnuts. Do a larger batch than what you'll need, and freeze the extra for future recipes.

4 cups water

1 tbsp. baking soda

3-4 cups raw hazelnuts

In a two to three-quart pan bring the water and baking soda to boil. Add the hazelnuts and cook for three minutes. Drain the nuts and immerse in cold water. Rub the nuts between your palms to loosen and remove the skins. Rinse the skins off the nuts and rub mostly dry with a towel.

Preheat oven to 300 degrees Fahrenheit.

Spread the nuts in a single layer on an ungreased, rimmed baking sheet (you don't want the nuts rolling off the pan), and bake for 8–10 minutes to dry them.

Remove baking sheet from oven to let the hazelnuts cool for at least 15 minutes. Return the nuts to the oven and bake for approximately 10 more minutes until they are toasted a golden brown. Shake the baking sheet occasionally to ensure an even toasting. Cool and use.

Hazelnuts can be refrigerated in an airtight container for up to a week or bagged and frozen.

MOCK DEVONSHIRE CREAM

Real Devonshire Cream is a thick, rich cream that originated in Devon, England. Found in gourmet and specialty shops and sold in small jars, Devonshire Cream is a traditional part of English cream tea and is served with scones and jam. The following recipe is our version of a substitute.

1 pkg. (3 oz.) cream cheese,
   softened

2 tbsp. powdered sugar

½ tsp. vanilla extract

⅓ cup heavy whipping cream,
   whipped

With an electric mixer, beat the cream cheese, powdered sugar, and vanilla extract together until smooth. Fold in the whipped cream, and chill until ready to serve. Makes approximately ¾ cup of cream mixture.

LEMON CURD

This spread can be a delicious addition to your scone-eating experience. It also makes a lovely gourmet gift from your kitchen.

2 large lemons

1 cup granulated sugar

4 large eggs, room temperature

pinch of salt

5 tbsp. unsalted butter, melted

Microwave the lemons for 30 seconds in the microwave (this will help them yield more juice). With a small knife or potato peeler, thinly pare the rind (yellow part only) from the lemons and set aside.

Halve the lemons and squeeze the juice into a small non-aluminum container. Strain the juice. Pour ½ cup of the juice into the top of a double boiler. Add the sugar, eggs, and salt and whisk the mixture until blended. Stir in the lemon rind and the melted butter.

Cook over, but not touching, simmering water. Constantly stir the mixture and scrape down the sides of the pan until the lemon curd thickens enough to coat the back of a wooden spoon. Do not let the mixture boil.

Strain the lemon curd through a fine sieve into a clean bowl to remove the lemon rind and any egg particles. Spoon into small, sterilized jelly jars, if desired. To prevent a skin from forming, cover with a sheet of plastic wrap and press onto the surface.

Store in the refrigerator for up to a month. Makes approximately 1½ cups of lemon curd.

MOM AND THE PIG

As a girl, my mother lived on huge self-sustaining farms and, later, in the big cities of St. Paul, Chicago, and Duluth. My father was from a small town in northern Minnesota near the Canadian border, and when they married and moved there, my mother found that her life would be lived in a primitive environment. Their home was a rustic cabin made of logs with a tar paper-covered roof. There was no electricity or indoor plumbing—not even running water in the kitchen. Water was hauled from my dad's brother's place down the road. During the cold northern winters, the house was heated by two wood-burning stoves: one the cook stove and the other a "heater" in the living room.

Determined to make the most of the situation, my mother made this homestead as self-sustaining as possible. My dad worked on the ore boats on the Great Lakes and was gone from ice breakup in the spring to freeze up in the fall, and so it fell to my mother to do all that she could do to sustain some semblance of prosperity on the property. In those days and in that place, people did not jump in the car and run to the store for items. They made their own and used things until they were used up.

Soon there was a herd of goats for milk and hutches of rabbits for meat. A garden of sorts was attempted despite the short growing season. Gooseberries and blueberries were gathered from the wild and canned. No one thought anything of the fact that when the jars of gooseberries were opened, the worms had to be skimmed off the top. Everyone made their own bread. In that house, with no electricity, clothes were washed in a copper tub of boiling water on the stove and dried outside on the line, even in the winter when they froze. Kerosene lamps illuminated the dark northern days.

Most people raised at least one pig each year, and I can remember going with my parents to pick out a young one from several in a slab wood enclosure with their mother. The men told me not to stand on the fence because the old sow would grab me, pull me in, and eat me. The pigs were almost wild, and this had indeed happened to one little girl. I suspect those tough frontier men were just as wild.

This was the routine for getting a little pig: The purchaser would decide on a pig and point it out. The owner would then fill the trough with food, and when the sow put her face down to eat, the owner would leap into the pen, quickly grab the little pig, and vault over the fence out of reach of the sow. As soon as the piglet started to squeal, the mother would try to come to its rescue. No one wanted to be bitten by a full grown pig!

One year my mother decided to raise piglets herself as a way of earning some cash. Somehow she sent for a purebred Chester White sow. The pig came in a crate on the train, and all the men who knew about its arrival thought my mom was crazy. Unlike her, they were used to the vicious razorback hogs. My mother did not care about what they said, though she knew that she was the "odd man out," having come from the city. She raised that pig carefully and with kindness, and she was rewarded with a batch of many little piglets born, of course, when it was cold. She saved them all by heating bricks in the oven, wrapping them in flannel, and putting them in the straw by the piglets. The goats were also in the barn, providing some warmth.

Everyday, as the piglets grew, Mom handled them and told the old sow what nice babies she had. Their squeals did not dismay the mother at all. When it came time to sell the pigs and men came to choose, they all snickered and laughed amongst themselves at the supposed pending spectacle of my mother vaulting over the fence with a squealing pig under her arm.

The men asked, "How do you expect to get those pigs out of there?" My mother, with a straight face, replied, "Well, I am just going to go in there and pick them up." That seemed like a crazy thing to the men, who were used to running for their lives while performing the same task. They gathered around the pen, expecting some real entertainment. Each chose the piglet he desired, but their hopes for a good laugh were shattered. With each sale, my mother calmly walked into the pen without baiting the sow with food, picked up a little one, and carried it out. As usual, the sow paid no attention to the squealing piglets.

The moral: Don't shrink from approaching a problem in a new way, even if others may not approve. Nothing says that we need to follow the pack. Planning, walking through a project ahead of time, and using common sense and logic can lead to benefits for all.

Rosalie Clarke

IDEAS FOR SHARING

Beautiful and delicious scones must be shared with others! Here are a few ways to share your scones with your family, friends, and neighbors. These ideas will help you celebrate their victories, make them feel at ease, lighten their burdens, and show your love and compassion for them. Be sure to come up with some ideas of your own too!

SCOTTISH SCONES

Line a basket or wooden bowl with a plaid cloth napkin and pile the scones inside. Give with a jar of homemade jam or a small container of creamed honey. *(Recipe on page 15.)*

BASIC BRITISH SCONES

Use pretty tea towel and a creamy-white vintage plate to present these scones. Include a small jar of lemon curd for an elegant touch. *(Recipe on page 18.)*

FRENCH APPLE-CREAM SCONES

Why not arrange these beautiful scones on a covered pedestal cake plate to give as a gift? Scones look good and disappear fast when they're under glass. *(Recipe on page 30.)*

MAPLE-WALNUT SCONES

Consider making this a cozy gift with warm-colored napkins, Maple-Walnut Scones, packets of gourmet hot chocolate, whole walnuts, and a fancy nutcracker. Arrange everything in a beautiful crockery bowl, wrap in cellophane, tie with a ribbon and make someone feel very special. *(Recipe on page 36.)*

DATE SCONES

Line the container of your choice with a nice tea towel. Add fresh apples, cheese, and the Date Scones. Include a nice wooden cutting board and new paring knife. Wrap in cellophane, tie with a ribbon and give as a thank you gift to someone who could use some appreciation. Be sure to include a handwritten note expressing your gratitude in specifics. *(Recipe on page 38.)*

CHERRY-ALMOND SCONES

A breakfast tray, new teapot and collection of herbal teas are some of the items that can be brought together to showcase Cherry-Almond Scones. Include an inspiring book or magazine and it becomes a gift designed to encourage a relaxing morning. *(Recipe on page 41.)*

APRICOT-GINGER SCONES

Help a friend de-stress by hand-delivering a charming basket or bowl filled with scones, packets of herbal tea and a small bouquet of colorful fresh flowers. *(Recipe on page 46.)*

HAZELNUT-RASPBERRY SCONES

Load a bowl, basket or other fun container with Hazelnut-Raspberry Scones and a variety of gourmet hot chocolate mixes. Include some sturdy mugs, tuck in a few ski scarves or hats and you have a perfect gift for enjoying a snowy day. *(Recipe on page 50.)*

STREUSEL SCONES

Our get-togethers don't have to be limited to dinner time. Invite family or friends over for breakfast or brunch and be sure to include Streusel Scones and All-Those-Raisin Scones on the menu. *(Recipe on page 59.)*

CHOCOLATE MUMBLE SCONES

The next time your teenager comes through the door with a horde of friends, offer "Mumbles & Milk" as a snack. Everyone will be delighted and you will have fun interacting with all those enthusiastic young people. Just make sure they put their dishes in the sink when they're done. *(Recipe on page 60.)*

DOUBLE CHOCOLATE-HAZELNUT SCONES WITH RASPBERRY FILLING

A few years ago while at a job interview, I was frankly told by the women interviewing me that their particular office "ran on chocolate." I later discovered this was absolutely true. The more stressful things became, the more chocolate everyone wanted. Help your office run more smoothly by sharing these scones with your fellow employees. Just be prepared. You'll get requests for more. *(Recipe on page 62.)*

"True [sharing] springs from right feelings; it is a good heart manifesting itself in an agreeable life; it is a just regard for the rights and happiness of others in small things; it is the expression of true and generous sentiments" (The Lady's Vase, 1843).

Happy sharing,

Beverly Pogue & Rosalie Clarke

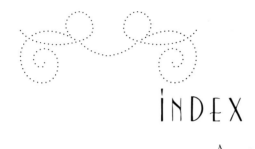

INDEX